BOOKS BY DONALD FINKEL

What Manner of Beast   1981

Going Under *and* Endurance   1978

A Mote in Heaven's Eye   1975

Adequate Earth   1972

The Garbage Wars   1970

Answer Back   1968

A Joyful Noise   1966

Simeon   1964

The Clothing's New Emperor   1958
(IN POETS OF TODAY VI)

WHAT MANNER OF BEAST

WHAT MANNER
OF BEAST

POEMS BY
DONALD FINKEL

Atheneum 1981 NEW YORK

The sources of the quotations incorporated in the poems are as follows:

THE STRANGE ONE—Hakluyt, Fox, Lok, Lok
THE GARDEN—Itard
THE NEGATIVE PARTICLE—both from Premack
PASSION IN PARADISE—both from Goodall
THE DOLPHIN AND THE LADY—Lilly
THE BEAST IN THE MACHINE—both from Rumbaugh
HIS NEED—all from Itard
ANOTHER MATTER—all from Frobisher
OF COURSE—Premack, Temerlin, *The New Yorker*
LUCY CAT—both from Temerlin
WHITE FOX—Hearne
MMMMMM—both from Howe
CHASE LUCY—Temerlin
THE LESSON FOR TOMORROW—both from Weir
BY OUR SIGNS—Hakluyt, Lok

Some of these poems, or versions thereof, have previously appeared in *Chowder Review, GiltEdge, Gramercy Review, Massachusetts Review, New England Review, Other Islands, Poetry Northwest,* and *Poetry Now.*

Library of Congress Cataloging in Publication Data

Finkel, Donald.
   What manner of beast.

   I. Title.
PS3556.I48W4 1981   811'.54   81-66012
ISBN 0-689-11226-2   AACR2
ISBN 0-689-11225-4 (pbk.)

for Washoe and the rest

There is no abyss between man and animals; the two domains are separated by a tiny rivulet which a baby could step over.

REMY DE GOURMONT,
The Natural Philosophy of Love

Everyone on earth feels a tickling at the heels; the small chimpanzee and the great Achilles alike.

FRANZ KAFKA,
A Report to an Academy

CONTENTS

WHAT MANNER OF BEAST

THE STRANGE ONE

1:

These strangers made offer of friendship, whereupon,
by signs, it was agreed that one of their men should
come in the skiff aboard the ship, while in pledge for
him, one of our men went on land.

MICHAEL LOK, *Account of Martin Frobisher's First*
Voyage to the Arctic

There is no accounting for strangers
preferring his bitter tea, his rancid fish
madeira fled down his imperturbable gullet, leaving
not the least flicker of approval

nor would he sit in the Captain's chair
but rapped it with his knuckles
stroked the table, fingered the pewter dish
touched his tongue to the lens of the Master's glass

They are greatly delighted with any thing that is bright,
or giveth a sound.

for beads, for tiny black fires
without smoke, without heat
for a pair of glasses, for wafers of moon
frozen so fast they will not come
unfrozen, even on his tongue
he would part with his parka

and a nail, for a threepenny nail
he would throw in his pipe
for iron, that bends without breaking
that keeps its edge, that holds
a finer point than bone

seeing Iron they could not forbeare to steal

for iron
that fixed him to fish-pale Kabloona
with a swarm of glittering hooks
he would part with his life

2:

the Captain did wisely foresee that these strange people
were not to be trusted

Next time the People hove into view in their great canoes
but would not come near, it was this same stranger
who eased his slim craft past the *Gabriel*'s chains
wherupon the Captain called for a little bell
and dangled it chiming over the side

but with a short arme

so that when the stranger reached for the music
his benefactor plucked him by the wrist
stunned, incredulous, kayak and all
out of the water and onto the deck
whereupon the People withdrew once more
to their barbarous hovels
and the Captain ordered the mainsails set

as for the stranger, he lived
till they landed in England
then died of a cold he had taken at sea

for a handsaw and a sailmaker's needle
his furs, his kayak, and his life
there is no accounting

in pledge for him I come at last
ambassador of sackcloth, envoy of ashes

4

paddling my wobbly conscience, I make for the shore
me for the strange one
him for me

RESOURCES

There is enough power in the scent of honeysuckle
to boil a three minute egg

a lover's sweat would serve to salt it
the buzzing of one fly against the pane

would keep the night-light burning in the nursery
there are springs we haven't begun to tap

if, outside the gates, an army of beggars
tugging ropes thick as a butcher's wrist

were to raise against the sky one run-of-the-wind-mill
if a detachment of bankers dug in their heels to steady it

if a legion of widows began to sigh
if a regiment of senators, a phalanx of chaplains

brayed and prayed
if a squadron of poets

the clumsy fans might creak and turn a stone
to grind the words to make the flour to bake the loaves

to feed one ravenous child
two thousand years

THE GARDEN

*in order not to sever him entirely from his country
tastes, he was taken continually to walk in some neigh-
boring gardens*

JEAN-MARC-GASPARD ITARD, *The Wild Boy of Aveyron*

Galumphing in his clumsy shoes
down rational cypress avenues
mown paths, raked gravel walks
between exemplary boxwood hedges
irreproachable topiary
borders of hollyhock and poppy
bedded and weeded, chaste and mannerly
the lush geometry of Luxembourg
that green decorum delighted and soothed him
ravished, tranquilized, enchanted
in the garden enclosed, the child set free

how was it then, when the cold wind moaned
Madame Guerin woke in the night
to hear from Victor's room upstairs
peals of sweet immoderate laughter?

*when the inclemency of the weather drove everybody
from the garden, that was the moment when he chose
to go*

one morning when she went to wake him, Madame
remembers turning the key, as ever
behind her in the lock, at the click she saw him
leap from bed with a tremulous cry
and run to the window, how was it then?

there had been in the night a fall of new snow
below, the garden stretched and yawned
in a shimmering peignoir edged with lace
the child ran laughing to the door

7

which held, she remembers, and once more
to the window, uttering tiny cries
like a captive bird, then suddenly
in the time it takes to make a wish
he was out the door and down in the garden
scampering barefoot in his nightshirt
tumbling through soft drifts, caressing the privet
shaking the fig tree, catching the blossoms
on his tongue, as the garden rang with laughter

how could she bear to call him back?

THE INVENTION OF O

When he found the kitten and called it *dog*
when he called the eagle *duck,* they thought
he'd made all the names he was going to make

when he crept to the moon-pool on hands and knees
and murmured to the swimming face, *baby*
when he said *fly* to a speck of dust, to his thumb
to a little toad, and the toad flicked its fabulous
tongue, unsaying a fly he hadn't seen

he lifted his head to the moon and called out, *O*
O, he called

THE NEGATIVE PARTICLE

Though Sarah found the negative an aversive word, she even asked: "What is an apple not?" and replied, "Bread."

DAVID PREMACK, *Intelligence in Ape and Man*

What is an apple Sarah?
spill it, is it *please fruit*
is it *sweet want* on the branch
trilling red cadenzas
or *goodbye Sarah* in the hand
what Dr. P calls a *contingent event?*

in the sequestered night
you take the words in your mouth
stroll to the board and propose
multi-colored plastic questions
spell out magnetized replies
caressing the words as you speak them
even the querulous *don't*

> *"No," or more credibly, "don't" was taught her simply by staying her hand whenever she reached for an item referred to in a sentence to which a negative particle was appended.*

in a garden of bolts and padlocks
Lucy mastered early
the mysteries of hook and key
the signs for *dirty* and *sorry*
Washoe signed a litany of *sorry*

> *frequently gestured "please sorry," "sorry dirty," "sorry hurt," "please sorry good," and "come hug sorry sorry."*

reaching for the apple, Lana glances
furtively at the technician

10

sensing the faint aversive tug
at forearm and wrist
caught in mid-flight, the tremulous act
in the talons of *thou-shalt-not*

THE MORNING THE ORCHID DECIDED TO BE A BUTTERFLY

Man can make a decision in an instant. The thought of
a plant might take 100 years.

ALFREDO BLAUMANN

What was the starweed pondering
the morning the orchid decided
to be a butterfly
as homo habilis lifted his flint
and struck at the underbrush?

what was the yarrow dreaming
the day grandfather Cain began
weeding his garden
what was the redwood about to say
when the chain-saw struck?

when the sunflower stammers into song
only the wheat will lend an ear
when the nettle frames a paean to the sun
only the queen-anne's-lace will smile

in the steamy green
the orchid lifts
its brittle wings
in hope of a breeze

THE ONE-EYED CAT

Stalking the stony terraces
dressed in nothing but my lives
it's height I need
I'm only happy out on a limb

june-wind licks white combers of boneset
and queen-anne's-lace
and spruces shrug their dust-blue shawls
and look away

a nestling dangles from my teeth
the grackles swoop and scream
nothing can touch me
but the wind

PASSION IN PARADISE

For reasons yet undetermined, in 1970 our main study community began to divide. Seven males and three females with offspring established themselves in the southern (Kahama) part of the home range.

JANE GOODALL, "Life and Death at Gombe"

And for reasons yet undetermined
not four years later, a gang of five
fullgrown Kasakela males from the north
caught a single Kahama deep in his own territory
and kicked and pummeled and bit him to death

and next month three Kasakelas did in another
prime Kahama male, then five slew Goliath
while four assaulted Madam Bee, without provocation
and left her daughter shooing flies from her wounds
five days, till she died

If they were merely trying to reclaim territory they had lost, they have certainly succeeded.

four years of search-and-destroy
and the southern range was liberated
though of the two Kahama females remaining, nothing is said
nor of their offspring, but it is presumed
the United Nations sent in a team of advisers

while for reasons yet undetermined
one Kasakela female, Passion by name
drove off her countrywoman, Gilka
made away with her infant and shared it with her daughters
tearing morsels from its breast
as though it were bush pig or monkey flesh

then Gilka's next-born, Passion's elder daughter
likewise kidnapped, and likewise equally shared
while forty-some armed rebels from Zaire

14

chugged quietly across the lake
and carried off four graduate students
for reasons equally unclear

> *It is sobering that our new knowledge of chimpanzee
> violence compels us to acknowledge that these ape
> cousins of ours are even more similar to humans than
> we thought before.*

Cain's not alone, beast among beasts
his deeds are deft and murderous as the shark's
his works, like the termite's, towering and transient
his most unnatural act is a freak of nature
malign as a tidal wave or a tornado

bad news from the garden at Gombe
the mark on Passion's brow is intelligence
deadliest of virtues
for rarely the fruit falls wide of the tree

THE ECOLOGIST'S NOTEBOOK

He records how seals weep copiously out of water
having beached themselves on his island
of their own accord

wax-wings, blue herons visit
and how, he wonders
do slender, fragile snakes like the ring-neck
reach such islands as his

they've sought him out as earnestly
as he seeks them
against all odds, against their sounder judgment

surrounded by seals, gulls, pollock, cunner, cod
a pod of fortuitous whales
he names from a handbook the fish in his traps
then guts them for supper

THE WORK OF AN INSTANT

For an instant I glimpse her
through the moonstruck tuna
milling and thrashing
she is composed now
under the jostling
one flipper snared in the senseless mesh

the lunatic silver curtain closes
beside me my father
breathless, half-spent
half the catch still to be stowed below
raises his bloody truncheon
his wet black hip-boots
gleam like a fearfully cloven tail

the wicked moonlight
winks at the tip of my grappling hook
as I plunge it into the frantic fabric
it's only the work of an instant
to free her

and lightyears before
I lose sight of her
sinking among gull-scraps
wearing the old imperturbable smile
unresisting, a goddess of garbage
the word made meat

SEAL SPELL

So you sank into the sun
and your fingers turned into
the innumerable seals

Eskimo Chant, EDWARD FIELD (*after Rasmussen*)

It was not we who drove away the salmon
it was not we who sent the caribou
back where they came from
where the bloody Chippewas feast
while our daughters yowl from the depths
of their swollen bellies

it was not we who stole your mother's breath
as she raised you up and sucked your nostrils clear
it was not we who left you yowling
on her icy breast, who led your father
into the night, it was not we
who sucked him down through the brash
filling his nostrils with ice

it was not we who pried you loose
from your mother's stiffening fingers, Nuliajuk
and set you in the kayak of death
it was not we who paddled you out to the deeps
who raised the skinning knife over your fingers
clutching the gunnel, who brought it down
painting the kayak redder than sunset

yet your fingers swam from the bloody knife
already darkening, already healing
yet we say it right out, we dare to say it
it is we who sing of you, orphan Nuliajuk:
Come back little fingers
we need you now

18

DOLPHIN EMBASSY

It is for this he was borne here, on a litter
to this kingdom of concrete
washed and tended, fed and fattened
where he waits, unblinking
bathing Margaret's ankles in a stream
of faint continual cries
as she glides from the shallows
like Aphrodite coming back
sea-water lapping her marble knees

murmuring endlessly *mammalmammalmammal*
to remind her where she comes from
where he comes from, her inscrutable hostage
she approaches the last of the lost tribes
her kissing cousin, Peter
uncanny as a black archangel
those dazzling flanks
that fixed archaic smile

THE DOLPHIN AND THE LADY

MARGARET: *say HELLO GOOD BOY   we are go-*
ing to speak
PETER: *cc   c   ccxxxxw   aw   xxx*
MARGARET: *English yet, Peter . . . say HUMAN-*
OID . . . HUMANOID
PETER: *xxxxxxxxx*

JOHN LILLY, *The Mind of the Dolphin*

All day, up to her knees in his element
she wades across the flooded room
with difficult grace
her sweet voice echoes in the salty nave
calling Peter to lessons
while creaking and croaking
whistling, farting
flooding the room in his genial stridor
he leaps, twirls, waltzing the water
on his tail, a grinning prince
in a concrete pool

> *to humans they sound raucous, derisive, impolite, even*
> *scatological, but at least very alien*

the lady tosses a golden ball
and warbles, *bring ball bring ball*
it's recess time in dolphin school

might as well teach stones to sing
teach the weeds to conjugate

THE BEAST IN THE MACHINE

*To provide social contact, it was first decided that an
orangutan, Biji, would live in the language-training situ-
ation with Lana.*

DUANE RUMBAUGH,
Language Learning by a Chimpanzee

Lana scowls at the keyboard
she knows why I call these plastic wafers *keys*
she wonders which one unlocks Biji
and where I have hidden the days of their ignorance
in this plexiglass Eden
tickling, grooming, hugging, sharing
tussling under the Guggenheim tree

> *she was both interfering with Lana's work on the key-
> board and restricting Lana's linguistic expressions to
> requests for the barest necessities*

Please machine give Coke
Please machine give M & M
sagely the monitor blinks, an electronic angel
a relay hisses in the wall
and there is Coke
dark, sweet, stinging her tongue with pleasure
click-click, there is M & M
wafer of eternal bliss, body of the machine
through the plexiglass the banked dispensers glow

but where has she gone
sweet orange Biji
silly irresistible Biji
dangling from the go-bar
brushing the console with her toes?

distracted, Lana taps out *Please machine make movie*
for 30 seconds of Primate Growth and Development

21

which she knows by heart
her genesis in technicolor
then it's back to the non-stop
night and day commercial of the dispensers

> *Quite possibly the various incentives such as movies
> had held little reward value for Lana as long as she had
> the companionship of another ape.*

Please machine open, she scans the console
for the key to *window,* for a glimpse of the action
east of Eden, in the alleys of Nod
where the technicians stray, white-robed and slim

between the hunger and the monkey chow
lies the machine
between the boredom and the colored slides
the machine, which once
toward morning, she entreated
Please tickle Lana

clapped in her plastic cage, tapping out
telegrams to the remote
elusive genius of the machine
her name and the machine's are one
all she needs is a lab coat and a Ph.D.

HIS NEED

I did not doubt that if I dared to reveal to this young man the secret of his restlessness and the aim of his desires, an incalculable benefit would have accrued.

JEAN-MARC-GASPARD ITARD, *The Wild Boy of Aveyron*

Three Sundays running, in the second year
Madame Guerin woke to hear him
crying in his room, no, calling
as a bird calls from his perch in the first
glimmer of false dawn, *lli lli lli*

three sounds the wild child learned
to fatten his orphan dialect
of mutter and grunt, chuckle and howl
first there was *O,* which he answered to
like a name, but couldn't bring himself
to say, then *lait,* an infant grace
the Doctor coaxed him to chant over milk
and now this warbling at the brink of light
this sweet unmeditated *lli lli lli*

how many Sundays was it, Julie
had joined them for dinner? her faultless Julie
of the downcast eyes, the forthright breasts
that could impale a saint, provoke
not a sound, but a psalm of longing
a song such as infant Solomon
might croon in his cradle, *Julie Julie*

> *I have seen him in a company of women attempting to relieve his uneasiness by sitting beside one of them and gently taking hold of her hand, her arms and her knees*

no more, that meek charade once over
he thrust her away and sought another
soft, recalcitrant shape, and another

23

till, gently taking hold of her hand
he drew one woman into the alcove
circled her pensively, then flung his arms round her
slender, sinewy, half savage, half boy

she was the last he ever touched
till the day of his death, but for Madame
and that was only when she had been
away too long, he'd cling to her
shuddering like a child who'd given up hope

> *this resignation has served only to exasperate him and*
> *has led the unfortunate creature to find nothing but a*
> *cause for despair in an imperious need*

for all the Doctor's soothing baths
and violent exercise, the storm
in Victor gathered, tossing him
from agony to grief to rage

one morning he sank his teeth in her hand
the tempest guttered like a candle
aghast, he knelt to kiss the wound
his wild heart fluttering in its cage
blood trickling thickly from nostril and ear

> *on the other hand, suppose I had been permitted to try*
> *such an experiment, would I not have been afraid to*
> *make known to our savage a need which he would have*
> *sought to satisfy as publicly as his other wants and*
> *which would have led him to acts of revolting indecency*

her husband dead these twenty years
her man-boy dead at forty-three
one week now, in the tiny house
Madame remembers, what was the pretext?
pressing her ear to Victor's door
remembers the latch-key turning slowly

so many years and lives ago
how, hunched on his bed, stroking his lonely
half-boy-half-man-root, he gazed
across the altar of his need

what does the Doctor know of need?
three times this week alone she's waked
in the empty house, to nothing at all
to a cry like a fishbone caught in her throat
Victor Victor Victor Victor

ANOTHER MATTER

1:

What knowledge they have of God, or what Idoll they
adore, we have no perfect intelligence. I think them
rather Anthropophagi, or devourers of mans fleshe then
otherwise: for that there is no flesh or fish which they
find dead (smell it ever so filthily) but they will eate it

Frobisher's account of his second voyage

From the first encounter, all escaped
but one, huddled in the forestays
scowling like a Tartar
in his bloody skins

now, from the last transaction
this old witch, lost in her furs
like a withered root
when the men first flung her to the deck
they tore her moccasins off to see
if her feet were cloven

very strange and beastly
maggots nuzzling the salmon
seal-guts spread on a stone to dry

bleeding from a scalp-wound, the younger female
croons over an injured girl-child, barely two
hugging to her meager breast, one arm
like a bloody doll

our Surgeon meaning to heale her childes arms, ap-
plyed salves thereunto. But she not acquainted with
such kind of surgery, plucked those salves away, and by
continual licking with her own tongue, not much unlike
our dogs, healed up the childes arme.

strange, strange
exceedingly strange
the mother's cheek tattooed in broad blue strokes
her lank locks glistening with blood

2:

> *The man Salvage formerly taken and she brought to-*
> *gether, every man with silence desired to behold the*
> *manner of their meeting, which was more worth the be-*
> *holding than can be well expressed*

A good space they beheld, each one the other
speechlessly, as if the grief of captivity
had riven their tongues

then the young female turned her face to the wall
and crooning, soft as a wounded dove
began to sing

> *as though she minded another matter*

Ice mother, your light
smiles from the snowcrust
winks at the sun

he trudges past you
brushing your hummocks
with his red knuckles

ice mother, mighty stillness
we drowse on your breast
the long night

through the skin
of your cold blue eye
we fish for our dinner

3:

but being again brought together, the Man broke up the
silence first, and with a sterne and stayed countenance,
began to tell a long solemne tale

Beside me, one brute fell
an arrow through the spleen
while, of the People, three
died on the beach

yet strove, while their arrows lasted
then gathered Kabloona's arrows
then snatched the arrows
from their wounds, and let those fly

and I saw, from the bow
of this demon canoe
an old man, bleeding
leap from the cliff

and another, I saw
then another, that they should not
be taken, leap
while the rest escaped

Whereunto she gave good hearing, and interrupted him
nothing till he had finished, and afterwards being
growne into more familiar acquaintance by speech, they
were turned together

and together, and together
each rarely out of the other's sight
as if they could not bear to be alone

yet never were they seen, in all that time
to use as man and wife
though she made his bed and dressed his meat

though she nursed him through his final illness
scrupulous as any Christian
she bathed him, crooning
her eyes turned to the wall

as though she minded another matter

OF COURSE

By the time of her fourth cycle, however, she twice attacked her previously favored trainers. The actual causes of the attacks are unknown of course

DAVID PREMACK, *Intelligence in Ape and Man*

When Sarah came into her fullness
she had been seven years from home
laboring in the rational vineyard
having not once laid eyes in all that time
on a male of her own persuasion
till Walnut, bright obliging Walnut, came

she reached through the bars
and clutching him close
took hs unfledged peter in her mouth
scrotum and all, whereupon
the trainer whipped out his clipboard and his Flair

For a brief period Walnut was used as a contingent event. On a board outside her cage we wrote such things as "Sarah is good ⊃ Mary give Sarah Walnut" and the more explicit "Sarah insert cracker red dish ⊃ Mary give Sarah Walnut." Instructions of this kind restored Sarah's work habits.

there are, of course, alternatives
take Lucy, who married a vacuum cleaner
when her labia bloomed, like some carnivorous flower
she dropped her magazine and plugged him in
ran his gleaming nozzle over her body
switching from SUCK to BLOW

until she had what I inferred to be an orgasm (she laughed, looked happy, and stopped suddenly). She then turned off the machine, picked up her unfinished glass of gin and her magazine.

30

or take the goose who courted the garbage can
three furious years, he defended his mate
from the garbage men, and danced the triumph dance
under her vacant, battered gaze
mounted her, in season
his wings, his heart aflutter

> *He would never react to greylag calls or even to fe-*
> *males, but if you'd just rattle a piece of metal he would*
> *immediately act as if there were another greylay calling*
> *him in the distance.*

when they carried his lady off for keeps
he watched them flatten her in the crusher
heard her death-rattle, then followed
the garbage-hearse, of course of course
two blocks through the deafening traffic
till he was crushed, himself

LUCY CAT

Her first response to the kitten was hostile; she tried to kill it. After several hostile introductions, the kitten suddenly started following Lucy and Lucy's attitude immediately changed. From that moment it became Lucy's cat.

MAURICE TEMERLIN, *Lucy: Growing Up Human*

Nor could she part with it, even
so it might eat, or if she did
could not forbear
to stroke it, as it lapped its cream
or sign to it, in the syntax of possession
Lucy cat, till at last it was sated

seven enchanted months, she trundled it
everywhere, a sentient toy
to practice love upon, or let it
ride her shoulders solemnly
pale angel tiger

   Unfortunately, though, one day the cat died.

crouched in the corner of her room
she crucified the afternoon
with screams like none she'd loosed before
then, suddenly struck dumb, approached
the incontrovertible tiny corpse
her forefinger not quite touching its fur
signing one long-drawn elegaic *you*

   She clearly had some understanding that the cat was
   dead, never to return, for she never looked for it again

learning in that instant the grammar of loss
never asked for it
nor uttered its name

till three months later, thumbing a magazine
she came on her image, peering from behind a tree
clutched to its bosom, limp, philosophical
Lucy's cat

an ape's age she stared mutely back
then started signing *Lucy cat* and *Lucy cat*
stroking with both hands sadly, over and over
imaginary whiskers, to which still clung
the frail dust-mice of recollection

IN THE VALLEY OF GIANTS

One greets me
not with its bony shoulder
nor its haunches, swathed in jay-blue cobwebs
but with a forepaw, naked and pink
like some forked enormous tongue
that nudges and nuzzles me
till I'm dizzy with welcome

kneeling, the better to groom me
it bends on me its importunate blue eyes
its ear-stumps cling to the sides of its head
like bewildered fungi

if only there were something I could say to it
beyond one brief appreciative purr

HOUND SONG

Three nights in a row
he fed on our leavings
rattling our cans
till we let him in

wherever we went, he went
to the end of his rope

we let him in
we let him out
we let him in again

one night at the corner, he paused
the old bones squared
his ears cocked soft to hear
what it said, it said
nothing I could hear

in the streetlight his life
hung loose on his bones
a hammock of shadow

we let him out
we let him in
we let him out again

WHITE FOX

*On seeing his countenance in a glass for the first time,
he exclaimed, "I shall never kill deer more," and im-
mediately put the mirror down.*

CAPTAIN JOHN FRANKLIN, *Narrative of a Journey to the
Shores of the Polar Sea*

He had not thought himself
so old

how his sinews sang
how his heart drummed
in its tent of ribs
as he thrust his fish-spear
at the tame one
there behind the hummock
where he was old enough
to be left when the others ran

there at Bloody Fall
where fifty years before
Sam Hearne's tame Chippewas
painted their shields and their faces
pulled off their stockings
tucked up their sleeves
entered in darkness five huts of the People
and butchered them down to the last infant
one joint at a time

five tents of the People
for a sack of tainted salmon
for a few lumps of copper
while Kabloona watched
groaning on his foundered feet

*Even to this day, I cannot reflect on the transactions of
that day without shedding tears.*

and when the tame one, smiling
fended the spear-thrust with his mitten
like so much snow
and brought Terreganook
White Fox, of the Deer Horn People
to his unsteady feet, at Bloody Fall
there at the brink of his narrow kingdom
caught between the Chippewas and the sea
it seemed to him only
it was an easy time to die

there in the lee of the hummock
drenched in the breath of fresh-thawed tundra
he had not thought
to find in this disc of miraculous ice
in this burnished slab of sun
his crumpled, waning, hopeless face

CARIBOU WOMAN

In my dream her black hands
beckon me through the snowlight
I hear them scrabbling on their scraggy nails
scraping ice from the heather

stumbling over the tundra
I saw one wrench a sprig from the permafrost
like a broken tooth
scored, scabrous knuckles of dwarf-pine
lashed by frost-scars
gnarled, charred, scarified
impervious to flame

afloat in my blue torpor
like a cloud over the cooking hut
I can see now through the smoke-hole
one crow-claw herding a wayward ember
back to the fold

the smoke-tongue licks my eyes, but I can see
the red stars dancing on her sooty shoulders
I can make her out now
flat on her belly like a wingless crow
breathing life into the fire

rousing me from my dream
her left claw gently scrapes my cheek
like a willow twig

gnawing the last of the rancid salmon
by the faltering light round the heather wick
afloat in the last of the caribou tallow
I watch her pluck a smoldering coal
to light her pipe

THE SCULPTOR'S GARDEN

Lately the horses won't nibble his grapes
the children won't climb his marble arbor
nobody comes any more to stroke his alabaster
cat, or listen to the basalt
crow in the welded hedge
but he goes on chiseling roses
whittling grass

taking out the gravel at night
he waves to the limestone owl on the wrought iron bush
though she doesn't give a hoot

RECONSTRUCTING THE WRECK

The elm steps into the clearing
bearing a wing in her arms
the wounded blade of a sky-blue knife

the irrepressible aspens skip down-hill
kicking the wheels before them
the elders hurry back from the orchard
carrying doors

a maple sapling straggles in
with a scrap of tail
a devil's-paint-brush touches up the numbers

boneset, in his white coroner's coat
probes the underbrush for vertebrae
whispering down in the pasture, milkweed and yarrow
stitch little rags of flesh

WEEDS

I have no quarrel with bindweed
when I was a boy
dandelion was king of the gypsies
grinning in the park
through his sooty teeth

nettle and milkweed
burdock, chicory

the weeds move in
an army of poor relatives
shouldering the gladioli

boneset, heal-all
meadowsweet, mother of aspirin

and the weeds move out
impudent garlic the Greeks
called Stinking Rose
chewed against drunkenness
head colds strangers worms the plague
misses her shiftless cousins

goat's-beard, sow-thistle
daisy and mullein

she sidles to the roadside
and sticks out her thumb

all through the winter goldfinch dines
at thistle's table

IN THE COUNTRY OF WEEDS
THE ONE-EYED CAT IS KING

Padding absently past treasuries of goldenrod
past the catnip mint, moonwhite in mist
turning a blind eye to the villainous nettles
the drunken sundew, the incorrigible clover
the insolent columbine, twitching his cap-and-bells
I amble down the proletarian ditches
sniffing the ragweed, winking at the chicory

PILGRIM'S PROGRESS

Safe in my fluorescent cell
elbows planted in that precious clutter
my *Thesaurus of Gesture,* my *Handbook of Weeds*
The Memoirs of Australopithecus
Intelligent Life in the Lithosphere
among folded poems and neglected letters
I fashioned question after question:
why was the first word?
who invented the pronoun?
what did the tree know in the first place?
where is the first place?

then, up by the barnyard under the bur oak
I sat like a goofy uncle while Nim
untied my shoes, unzipped my fly
and sucked on my Flair

and now, as he slips his gritty confident
five-year-old hand in mine to draw me
down to the cottonwoods, scuffing barefoot
leaving a wake of baked red dust, what's that
my genes are muttering to one another?
I feel them quiver on their spindles
what do they want me to ask this urchin
beyond *what that* and *tickle where?*

WHAT MANNER OF BEAST

*From her first days on the island, Washoe signed to her
fellow chimps. Indeed, she signed to every person within
eyeshot, mostly with instructions to take her off the
island.*

EUGENE LINDEN, *Apes, Men, and Language*

Regarding from the boat the creatures
astraddle the sitting-poles, you sign
black bugs

no no, chuckles Roger
shipping the oars, *those chimps
those chimps there,* scratching his ribs
the same as for *monkey*
but higher

what manner of beast, you wonder
stares back at you, blank as a cat
at the old reliable *gimme banana*
at *please gimme berry*
and stealthily pops another raisin in his mouth

come hurry Roger
you semaphore madly
from the roof of the rundevaal
nobody answers

till, Washoe-wise
you give off begging
and sign to one stranger, *come hug*
then fling your arms round him

in a week there are two of you
signing and hugging
hugging and signing

THE BUSINESS IN HANDS

Washoe is to be an emissary from humanity, a Prometheus to chimpanzees

EUGENE LINDEN, *Apes, Men, and Language*

Hunched in the stern, across the moat
she carried speech, an ember seething
in her hands

hostage to science, her captors kind
within reason, nothing personal
three squares, her run of the scrub
and infinite leisure, perched on her sitting-pole
like a simian Simeon

let the doctors read their gloomy prognoses
in microslices of her liver
let the learned journals gnaw her name

it was time to get on with the business in hands
fumbling the gordian riddles of *who* and *what*
undoing the koan *look*
stroking the mantra *sweet sweet sweet*

A DIFFERENT DRUMMER

Nim's use of play *was by no means limited to humans.*

HERBERT TERRACE, *Nim*

At the end of August, under his tree
the gathered teachers began, like children
to clap their hands in unison
till, poised in the leafage, Nim began
to clap, perhaps to a different drummer

then clapping still, the chimp came down
descended among them, danced clapping away
as if the beast might teach his teachers

one climbed to her feet to follow, clapping
whereupon he paused, rolling onto his back
signing *tickle* and *come*

thereafter, precisely in that manner
bringing his hands together smartly
the ape signed *play* to cats and teachers
children and horses, without respect
to age or station

MMMMMM

*I am completely vulnerable to him and he pushes and shoves
my legs and feet, and quite pathetically tries to satisfy him-
self. I can feel his mounting frustration.*

MARGARET HOWE, in John Lilly's *The Mind of the Dolphin*

All night the lady tosses in her sodden sheets
shedding her own salt tears on the briny pillow
all night Peter's tail whap-whaps the water
restless wavelets twitch the flimsy curtain
uneasy shadows flounder on the ceiling
her ankles sting from the nicks of his teeth
but for all her human guile and feminine wit
it's Peter who teaches and Margaret who's taught

playing, he lets his favorite ball
roll back in his mouth, parting his teeth
in a permanent smile, as if to say
Come I won't hurt you

> *I stand very still, legs slightly apart, and Peter slides his
> mouth gently over my shin. His mouth opens all the way
> and he begins up and down my leg. Then the other leg.*

a month of this salty courtship
till one evening, in the second moon
of their togethering, he lets the ball
slip from his mouth entirely
and, rolling on his side
approaches

MARGARET: *MMMMMM MMAGRIT   Yes! Yes!*
(*clapping*) *That's*
PETER: (*softly*) *Mxx   xxx*
MARGARET: *an EM. Let's do it again. Say . . .*
MMAGRIT
PETER: *mxxxxxxxxx*

CHASE LUCY

Chase Lucy.
Not now.
Hug Lucy hurry hurry.
In just a minute.
(laughing) Hurry hurry hurry hug Lucy tickle chase.

MAURICE TEMERLIN, *Lucy: Growing Up Human*

My clipboard calls like a siren
only the work of an instant
to check on the List of Reliable Signs
the concepts *baby, banana, come-gimme*
more, open and *please*

> *Although she could easily outrun us, she almost never*
> *runs so fast that we cannot catch her*

the clip bears down on my life
like a trap long sprung
but she's smiling over her shoulder
wearing her grandest play-face
calling me to touch-tag and keep-away
wrestling, dress-up, blind man's bluff

not to the tournament of conversation
noun against steel-blue noun
this which-is red against *contingent event*
but to a round of catch, tossing
the airy red-and-yellow verb *come-hug*
between us, between apostrophes
of silent laughter, rollicking adjectives of teeth
hugging ourselves and each other
hurry, she signs to me
fluttering those ecstatic hands
while from under the clip the seconds
trickle from my side like rills of blood

THAT LISTEN

Lucy was making a pant-greeting when she saw me. She signed out Lucy. I asked who? and she signed Roger out Lucy. I unlocked her cage & went into the kitchen where I had started the tea. She signed out tea.

ROGER FOUTS, *unpublished notes on teaching Lucy to sign*

She takes me through the rite like a priestess
cherishing each gesture, attending
the blue prophetic flame, the enchanted kettle
announcing gravely, *tea go* and *Roger drink*
bidding me *swallow Roger,* obedient
I lift the fragrant cup to my lips

it's time for catechism
I bring her a radish, fruit of the ground
and begin, *what that?*
she bites and spits and signs back *cry hurt food*
signs *drink fruit* to a slice of watermelon
to a sweet pickle, *that pipe candy*
and whatsoever Lucy calls it
that is the name thereof

now it's Lucy's turn
she signs *what that?* to my watch
and I answer, *that listen*
nodding, she scrawls her signature
on the data sheet with my Flair
under New Sign Training

at my back, the kettle's keening litanies
the seconds scuttle through my Timex crystal
like fugitives, while under my pen
the word-list whispers, *listen listen*

let my novitiate begin
teach me the rites of kindliness
I'm beginning to listen, Lucy
I'm learning to learn

THE LESSON FOR TOMORROW

what color . . . what color blanket . . . what color
map . . . what color glass . . . what color TV . . .
red ant . . . fire . . . like lipstick . . . blanket . . .
now the blue blanket

Ruth Weir, *tape of a 2½ yr. old boy in his crib*

Repeating patiently the original question, *why?*
why? why? he coaches his mama in the art
of inquisition, *because fish have wings,* she answers
why? because it's Sunday, she's getting the knack of it
why? because, why? eat your why, good girl
why? because it's good for you that's why

he beams on his dear neophyte, benificent
the lesson is over, it's time for a spell
of small talk with his crib

mamamama with daddy . . . milk with daddy . . .
OK . . . daddy dance . . . daddy dance

reciting to the rapt night-light
the timeworn catechism of mamadaddy
then he'll run through the chapters of color
the verses of fire, for truly tomorrow
he'll edify them

hi daddy . . . only Anthony . . . daddy dance

truly tomorrow he'll take them
through their changes, but now
the blue blanket

51

AFTER RAIN

The house lies dripping like a stranded ark
the briar tries once again to climb to her knees
the eyes of rain are trembling in her hair

high in the forepeak, the mockingbird proposes
theme on theme of woodlark, grackle, vireo
the cardinal sings sweet ease sweet ease in the mock-orange tree

the jays trail their electric shrouds from limb to limb
spinning a web of clear blue noise
in which I quiver like a dancing fly

at the curb
the violets gather
waiting their turn

SUN UP

Light creaks
cracking the night
and pours the sun
in the valley's bowl
like a perfect yolk

clouds graze the horizon
mildly, sparrows
wake in the elms
unwinding skeins
of thready mist
as day-flower lifts
his blue unblinking
weather eye

his roots hold earth
so loose, the least
breath would set him
soaring free
kissing the thistles
skimming the common-
wealth of weeds
buzzing the apartments
of the honey bees

the earthworm strolls
through morning loam
brushing his lips
on the roots of light

THE APE WHO PAINTED

Toward the end of his painting career, Congo was producing excellent circles, but nearly always filled them in immediately.

ALEXANDER ALLAND, JR., *The Artistic Animal*

Toward the end the painter was subject to sudden
fits of aimless pacing, sucking the end of his brush
his lips were permanently Indian Red, a pigment
to which he had grown obsessively partial

from time to time he would pause
to examine an apple, turning it
in his long, sensitive fingers, or fish
a dust-mouse gently from under his bed
not a hair displaced
or moon for hours, sprawled on his favorite tire
praying to his thumb

how fortunate we are to have captured on film
this miraculous thumb, in full career
sweeping in a great assured arc from left to right
trailing a gleaming Indian Red parabola
counterclockwise, following its own law
tailing up again, toward its beginning
deftly dividing out from in
then filling carefully the bowl of zero
with precious red, horizon to horizon

toward the end, the painter's cage was strewn
with fallen suns, great bloody periods
pages from some cosmic calendar
while he grew more taciturn than ever

54

WHALE CANTICLE

The song appears to be evolving.

ROGER PAYNE, *Humpbacks: Their Mysterious Songs*

Late March, the last vast shapes appear
grazing the pack off Cape Adare
sifting the dark all austral summer
ruminating the same long thought

as the new green rubbery ice appears
in the indigo lanes, one matriarch
muses, how nice it must be north
this time of year at Barrier Reef
it's barely a month before she blows

in the chill grey noon her spume appears
to hang an instant, glimmering dimly
a bush of needles on the long low swell

by May on the Reef fat calves appear
cavorting in the rings their mothers make
their elf-cries lapped by the widening rings
of the song, as one by one they all
take up where they left off last year

wrapped in that music, some appear
to be keeping time with their barnacle-
crusted flippers, but never together
each in her own sweet time, now one
perfects the second theme, another
tries it on, as the canticle
takes shape in the warm blue wave, how nice
they never get all of it right at once

WASTE

By his guttering wick, the eskimo
strokes with a scrap of caribou hide
the flanks of a burnished ivory bear
slowly the beast begins to glow

even the hammer's stolid face
warms, as the carpenter warms to his task
whose forebears pressured blades of flint
so thin they sliced through April mist
and broke on flowers

no labor is ever lost—the years
rise through the ardent carpenter's roof
shimmering in waves of waste
deep in the steel the atoms dance
beyond the storm, the solemn bear
begins his dance among the stars

MOCKINGBIRD CANTATA

A jay's here, here
comes a cardinal, one
fat robin, fooling
neither other robins
nor myself, look out
for the auk, for the auk!

I'm shameless, a nightingale
of weeds, I know, a cardinal
could say it better in his sleep
an unfledged jay
screams more sweetly than I

but I run through thirteen breezy
versions from my aluminum
balcony without missing a beat
while the jay goes on complaining
while the sparrows natter, only
the other mockingbirds
are mute

WIND SONG

Button up brother
wind sang, I feel
like paying the rent!
then he kicked up his heels
and took off for the territories
bellowing gleefully
lashing his spindrift tail

then why all these hymns to stillness
these fugues of silence, cataleptic odes?
the dry twigs caper in his mane
the dust and the dead leaves
dance at the sight
even the stones are a little high

WEED MUSIC

Sunlight thrumming on a stone
makes it shudder in the weeds
wakes the cricket in its shadow

all across the field
stones dance and crickets sing
this is what the weeds call music

on the high wire
now the mockingbird
runs through his changes
whistling in nineteen languages
including Druid
tries on the cardinal's crest
the robin's bib, the jay's
skyblue pajamas
and leaps a dozen
feet in the air
still carrying on

the stones are humming
the crickets trip the light
the trees applaud

BY OUR SIGNS

The stones of this supposed continent with America be
altogether sparkled, and glister in the Sunne like gold:
so likewise doth the sand in the bright water.

HAKLUYT, *The English Voyages*

The dolphin in the plastic hammock
has learned to gurgle *Good morning*
Doctor Lilly through his spiracle
the ape Washoe has learned to curse
in fluent semaphore
by their signs we shall know them

waiting for a sign of the prodigal five
who'd vanished, rowing the *Gabriel's* skiff
round the stony point
for a sack of sparkle
a fistful of glister

They are greatly delighted with any thing that is bright

all day the Captain held at anchor
all eyes scouring the shore
and next morning, sailing close as he dared
to the cannibals' camp, he sounded
the *Gabriel's* trumpet, fired off a cannon

by his signs, unequivocal
by his trumpet and gun, they knew him
there rose from the huts
an answering blare of laughter

very strange and beastly

and the Captain swore never again
to make peace with those savages
spoke, from that hour
only the language of reprisal
the laying-on of arms

by our signs they shall know us
I pluck a louse from Washoe's fur
and crack it with my teeth
I swim out, flapping my black plastic tail
crying *Uncle, Uncle*
in clicks and squeals

SHHH

Listen, shhh
alone among trees
I've come for a heart-to-heart
with the woods
I fall on my knees
for a tête à tête with a geode

behind his limestone brow I sense
the clean hard corners of his thought
facet to facet, glinting dimly
postulates of amethyst and quartz

it's small talk time
I'll parley with the loam
make peace with the Indian Pipe
I'll learn to speak weedish

DONALD FINKEL was born in New York City and attended public schools there, notably the Bronx High School of Science. He studied sculpture at the Art Students League, and after earning a B.S. in philosophy and an M.A. in English at Colombia left the east for Illinois, Iowa, and finally St. Louis, Mo., where he is Poet in Residence at Washington University. He has lived for several years in Mexico, and travelled widely in the United States. He is married and has three children, three cats, and a Border Collie.

He is the author of *The Clothing's New Emperor* (1959), *Simeon* (1964), *A Joyful Noise* (1966), *Answer Back* (1968), *The Garbage Wars* (1970), *Adequate Earth* (1972), *A Mote in Heaven's Eye* (1975) and *Endurance* and *Going Under* (1978). He has been the recipient of a Guggenheim Fellowship and a grant from the National Endowment for the Arts. In 1974 he received the Theodore Roethke Memorial Award for the book-length poem, *Adequate Earth*. In 1980 he received the Morton Dauwen Zabel Award from the Academy and Institute of Arts and Letters for *Endurance* and *Going Under* (1978).